MANIFESTOS FOR THE 21ST CENTURY

SERIES EDITORS: URSULA OWEN AND JUDITH VIDAL-HALL

Free expression is as high on the agenda as it has ever been, though not always for the happiest of reasons. Here, four distinguished writers address the issue of censorship in a complex and fragile world where people with widely different cultural habits and beliefs are living in close proximity, where offence is easily taken, and where words, images and behaviour are coming under the closest scrutiny. These books will surprise, clarify and provoke in equal measure.

Index on Censorship is the only international magazine promoting and protecting free expression. A haven for the censored and silenced, it has built an impressive track record since it was founded 35 years ago, publishing some of the finest writers, sharpest analysts and foremost thinkers in the world. In this series with Seagull Books, the focus will be on questions of rights, liberties, tolerance, silencing, censorship and dissent.

Without ███████

███luding religious orthodoxies, it ceases to exist. La████

ion cannot be imprisoned, or art will die, and with it, a little of what ma

is human. What is freedom of expression? Without the freedom to offend

ceases to exist. Without the freedom to challenge, even to satirise all ortho

es, including religious orthodoxies, it ceases to exist. Language

and the imagination cannot be imprison

or art will die, and with it, a little of

what makes us human. What is freedom of expression

Without the freedom to offend, it ceases to exist. Without the freedom to c

enge, even to satirise all orthodoxies, including religious orthodoxies, it

ceases to exist. Language and the imagination cannot be imprisoned, or

███████████████████

ression? Without the freedom to offend, it ceases to exist.

s freedom of expression? Without the freedom to offend, it ceas

Without the freedom to challenge, even to satirise all orthodoxies, includ

religious orthodoxies, it ceases to exist. Language and the imaginat

cannot be imprisoned, or art will ███████████████

what makes us human. What is freedom of

expression? Without the freedom to offend, it ceases to ex

Without the freedom to challenge, even to satirise all orthodoxies, includ

religious orthodoxies, it c███████

be imprisoned, or art will die, and with it, a little of what makes us hum

is freedom of expression? Without the freedom to offend, it ceases to
om to challenge, even to satirise all orthodoxies, in-
ng religious orthodoxies, it ceases to exist.

CENSORING *the body*

Without the freedom to challenge, even to satirise all orthodox-
ncluding religious orthodoxies, it ceases to exist. Language and the
ination cannot be imprisoned, or art will die, and with it, a little of wha
s us human. What is freedom of expression? Without the freedom to of-
it ceases to exist. Without the freedom to challenge, even to satirise all
us orthodoxies, it ceases to exist. Language and

makes us human. What is freedom of expression? Without the
edom to offend, it ceases to exist. *Without the*
om to challenge, even to satirise all orthodoxies, including religious or-

EDWARD LUCIE-SMITH
What is

om of expression? Without the freedom to offend, it ceases to exist. With-
ie freedom to challenge, even to satirise all orthodoxies, including reli-
and the imagination cannot be
it, a little of what makes us human.

Without the freedom to challenge, even to satirise all orthodoxies, in-
uage and the imagina-
annot be impris... with it, a little of what makes
man. What is freedom of expression? Without the freedom to offend, it
s to exist. Without the freedom to challenge, even to satirise all orthodox-
ncluding religious orthodoxies,

Seagull
BOOKS
LONDON NEW YORK CALCUTTA

and with it, a little of wha
s us human. What is
it ceases to exist. Without the freedom to challenge, even to satirise all
uage and

Seagull Books

Editorial offices:

1st Floor, Angel Court, 81 St Clements Street
Oxford OX4 1AW, UK

1 Washington Square Village, Apt 1U
New York, NY 10012, USA

26 Circus Avenue, Calcutta 700 017, India

ISBN-10   1 9054 2 253 9
ISBN-13   978 1 90542 253 1

British Library Cataloguing-in-Publication Data
A catalogue record for this book is available
from the British Library

Typeset by Seagull Books, Calcutta, India
Printed and bound in the United Kingdom
by Biddles Ltd, King's Lynn

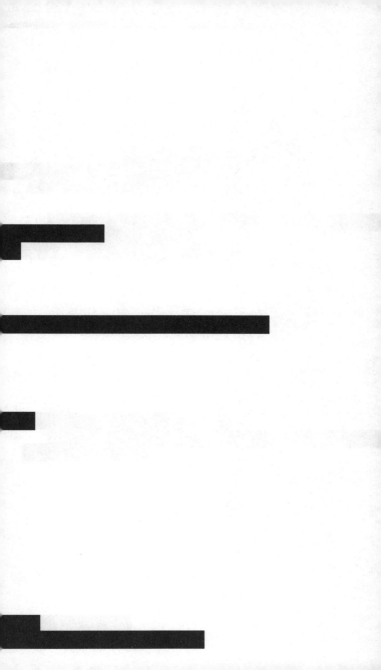

Our body is a battleground. Through history and across cultures, those with the power to do so—religious and secular leaders both—have denied our right to a full and frank portrayal of our bodies and their functions. But from the dawn of history, it seems, we, too, have colluded in the cover up.

EARLY CIVILIZATIONS

From the earliest times, human beings have found it difficult to represent their own bodies in a straightforward way. The rare painted images of humans in Palaeolithic art are much less naturalistic than the images of animals created at the same epoch. At the dawn of art, representations of the nude body were simply vehicles for statements about the need for fertility if the human race was to survive successfully. Both Palaeolithic and Neolithic sculptures tend to present human males and females in terms of exaggerated sexual characteristics. The *Venus of Willendorf* is one of the best-known Palaeolithic examples. The recently discovered Hongshan Neolithic-to-Chalcolithic culture that flourished in northeastern China and adjacent regions of

The female body reduced to a pair of
breasts and a vulva in a statue from the
Hongshan Neolithic-to-Chalcolithic period.

Mongolia from c.3500 BC to c.2000 BC produced numerous jade statues and amulets
that emphasize the sexual aspect. In some
of these the female body is reduced to a
pair of breasts and a vulva.

The emphasis on sexuality seems to have
reversed itself only when matriarchal forms of
religion began to be replaced by patriarchal
ones. Ancient Near Eastern civilizations were
noticeably prudish about representing the
unclothed body. This prudishness was inherited by the monotheistic religions rooted in
the Near East—by Judaism and by Judaism's
offshoots, Christianity and Islam. In their
strictest forms both Judaism and Islam impose a complete ban on the representation of
the body.

The Ancient Egyptians were a little less
strict in their attitudes, though it is noticeable, for example, that where male geni-

talia are shown in Egyptian sculpture they are usually reduced in size. Among the few exceptions are images of the fertility god Min, who is shown with an enormous phallus. These conventions were carried over into Greek Archaic and Classical art. When we look at Greek sculptures of the Classical epoch, at images by or derived from Phidias and Praxiteles, we are often struck by the fact that, in images of the male, the genitals are noticeably under-sized—this in spite of the Greek emphasis on heroic male nudity. The same observation can be made about Greek vase paintings, where the only male figures with large genitalia are those that are only marginally human—satyrs and pigmies for example.

About the only celebrated Greek statue with completely naturalistic, normal-sized sexual equipment is the Hellenistic—or

Praxiteles' *Aphrodite of Cnidus.*

copied-from-Hellenistic—*Dying Gaul* in the Capitoline Museum in Rome. No reason is ever suggested for this deviation from a by-that-time long-established convention, but it may be because the personage represented was, in Greek terms, a 'barbarian'. Nevertheless, in both Greek art and Roman art, representations of male genitalia had both a cult significance, as in images of the fertility god Priapus, and, as in numerous surviving phallic pendants, an apotropaic one.

Images of the female developed somewhat differently. In Archaic Greek art, the *kore*, or maiden, was always shown elaborately clothed, while the *kouros*, or youth, was shown naked. Nude females do appear in fifth-century Greek vase painting, but the body-types of young women often seem to be subtly assimilated to those of adolescent

boys. The nude female in three dimensions
was essentially a creation of the fourth century BC, with Praxiteles' *Aphrodite of Cnidus*
as the defining work in a new style. Though
the *Aphrodite* has great erotic impact, as be-
fits its subject, it offered, so far as we can
tell from surviving copies, no very specific
information about the female genital area,
which the goddess modestly covers with her
hand. This admission of shame about total
exposure makes a significant contribution
to the erotic effect made by the sculpture.
The fact that sexuality is here simultane-
ously revealed and concealed was something that was to have a long post-classical
history in Western art.

One non-European culture that offers a
striking contrast to these developments is
Hindu art in India. The Chandela temples

of Khajuraho in central India, built in the tenth century AD, offer a stunningly explicit series of sexual representations. While there is still controversy about the precise meaning of these sculptures, the consensus is that they symbolize a union with the divine. And while they are informative, even rather didactic, about various methods of sexual intercourse, they are not, in fact, particularly naturalistic. The copulating bodies are constructed from standard, semi-abstract elements and avoid what might seem too much individualized or specific.

Much the same thing can be said of the contemporary or slightly later Chola bronzes made in Tamil Nadu under the dynasty of that name. Even when these are not equipped with animal heads (as in

A Chola bronze of Siva.

representations of Ganesh) or additional limbs, the bodies are subtly stylized in ways that set them apart from what we see, or think we see, in the real world. In other words, they have been 'censored' to make sure that we know that these are representations of the divine, not of our own imperfect humanity.

CHRISTIANITY AND THE BODY

With the coming of Christianity, representations of the nude became associated with the idea of the Fall of Man and original sin. This, however, conflicted with the need to show nude or nearly nude bodies when representing episodes from Genesis, the Passion of Christ and the martyrdoms of popular saints, such as St Sebastian. Genesis was a particularly crucial text, because

nudity and shame about nudity play such
an important role in the story. Nudity represents innocence. Awareness of nudity
represents sin. In Late Antiquity, artists
were already losing the secure grip on bodily forms that had characterized developed
Greek art, and which had been inherited
by the Roman artists, largely Greek
trained, of the late Republican and early
Imperial epochs. They increasingly tended
to reduce all representations of the human
body to linear rather than fully plastic for-
mulations. Nevertheless, medieval art of
the eleventh, twelfth and thirteenth centuries offers some striking presentations of
the nude. One of the most celebrated is the
Romanesque relief showing a reclining Eve
by Giselbertus of Autun, which, despite its
schematic anatomy, retains a considerable
erotic charge.

Romanesque relief showing a reclining Eve by Giselbertus.

The element of the forbidden is
stressed in certain medieval representations
that exist on the margins of high art—in
the case of certain illuminated manuscripts,
quite literally so. These deliberately flout all
laws of decorum. Among the best-known of
these images are the so-called *Sheela-na-gig*
carvings to be found in churches, and
sometimes also on secular buildings, often
in the form of figurative corbels. Most
prevalent in Ireland, as the Gaelic name
implies, these are also found in other parts
of the British Isles and in Scandinavia.
They show a woman, often old and ugly,
who is aggressively exposing her vulva.
There has been much modern debate about
the meaning of these images, which are
sometimes seen as pagan survivals. This
appears to be the case in a general sense,
rather than a specific one: the exposed

A *Sheela-na-gig* carving.

vulva possesses the same apotropaic significance—the power to ward off evil—that was
attributed to the phallic pendants worn in
pagan antiquity.

With the coming of the Renaissance the
relationship between the sacred and the
profane, Christianity and the body, became
increasingly complex. Through the study of
the Antique, and also thanks to their own
observations, Renaissance artists, first in
Italy, then elsewhere in Europe, were able
to present the human form in a more and
more nuanced and realistic fashion. There
were, however, some oddities about this
progression. In the first place, anatomical
studies based on the dissection of corpses,
avidly pursued by leading artists such as
Leonardo da Vinci, were frowned on by the
Church, which paradoxically regarded the
human body as an inviolable temple, not to

be cut into fragments by eager anatomists, just as much as it was a temptation to and an occasion for sin. They therefore long retained a sulphurous reputation. Such studies did, nevertheless, have a lasting impact. The Greek notion of the 'ideal' body, conceptualized rather than seen with objective accuracy, became more and more difficult to sustain.

Second, the Church disapproved of the use of nude female models in studio situations where all the artists were male. This led to the curious practice, in the earlier years of the sixteenth century, of using young male apprentices—*garzoni* as they were called—to pose for female figures, such as that of the Madonna. Evidence of this way of working can be found in a number of Raphael's drawings.

Interest in antiquity and in pagan sto-
ries of all kinds, nevertheless led to the creation of an increasing number of images of
nude females. Botticelli's *Birth of Venus*,
painted in c.1483, is perhaps the most celebrated example from the earlier years of
the Renaissance. The figure is nude, but
not at all realistic: there is a deliberate de-
nial of rational spatial construction, and the
figure itself is deliberately flattened and
stylized, floating against the front plane of
the picture. It makes a striking contrast
with Titian's *Venus of Urbino*, painted just
over half-a-century later, in 1538. This
shows a beautiful nude woman reclining on
a bed. She gazes frankly at the spectator,
while her left hand touches her pubis, ca-
ressing it rather than actively concealing it.
In the background, two fully clad females
rummage in a chest.

The *Venus of Urbino* was a princely com-
mission from Guidobaldo II della Rovere,
Duke of Urbino, supposedly intended as an
instructive image for the very young bride
whom the duke had recently married.
Whether or not this was the case, it belongs
to a group of Renaissance nudes that oc-
cupy a special position in the societies for
which they were created. Examples can be
found throughout Europe, not just in Italy.
Other examples can be found in the deco-
rations that François I of France commissioned for his palace at Fontainebleau and
the *Venuses* and *Judgements of Paris* painted
by Lucas Cranach the Elder for successive
Electors of Saxony.

The Electors of Saxony were among the
most important patrons of the Protestant
cause, and Cranach was friendly with the

great religious reformer Martin Luther, whose portrait he painted in 1529. Since Protestantism is associated with the repression of all forms of erotic imagery, it is at first sight surprising to find such a considerable production of images of this type coming from Cranach's studio. In fact, princely commissions for art of this type seem to have been a subtle assertion of secular power. The ruler who took pleasure in and displayed such things was offering evidence that his elevated position in the social structure made him, to some extent at least, independent of the religious sanctions that could be enforced on lesser beings.

The invention of printing and the increasingly wide dissemination not only of printed texts but of printed images, created

a kind of hierarchy of censorship. Prints
were increasingly often the vehicle for
erotic representations that were much
bolder than anything that could be displayed in public. The most famous example
in the High Renaissance period is the series
of erotic prints entitled *I Modi*, showing
various sexual positions. These were
illustrations to extremely forthright erotic
verses by Pietro Aretino, and were the work
of Raphael's chief pupil Giulio Romano,
engraved by Marcantonio Raimondi. They
caused an enormous scandal when they
were published in 1524, not least because
they seemed to satirize various members of
the Papal court.

Other prints, almost as forthright,
slipped by pretty much unnoticed, and
were widely circulated and enjoyed; the

point being that they were easy to conceal,
and could be enjoyed in private, not in public. The artists concerned developed an increasingly elaborate symbolic language that
conveyed erotic meanings through indirec-
tion. A good and, as it happens, very early
example of this is Albrecht Dürer's woodcut
The Men's Bath of 1497. Without showing
overt sexual activity, this is full of references
to homosexual attraction. For example,
though all the men wear minimal loin
cloths, one leans against the pump that sup-
plies the bath in such a way that the large
tap protruding from it forms a more-than-
adequate substitute for his own concealed
genitalia. Another figure, in the centre of
the composition, plays the flute. In the context, and given the direction of his gaze,
which is directly towards the tap, his action
makes a sly reference to *fellatio*.

Albrecht Dürer's *The Men's Bath* (1497).

The conflicted feelings of Renaissance society concerning the ways in which the human body could or should be represented can, however, be found in almost every aspect of the art of the time. Art did not have to be secular to carry a powerful erotic charge. Perhaps the most striking instances of this are Michelangelo's frescos in the Sistine Chapel, in particular the huge *Last Judgement* (1541) that occupies the whole of the east wall above the altar. By the time the composition was completed, the Roman church was beginning to absorb many of the repressive attitudes towards overt sexual expression that already typified Protestantism. Because many of the figures were nude the painting became the subject of a violent campaign by members of the *curia*, notably Cardinal Carafa, to have these obliterated or censored. Pope

Paul III's Master of Ceremonies, Biagio da Cesena, described the figures in *The Last Judgement* as being more suited to a bath-house than a chapel. Michelangelo promptly included him in the composition as Minos, the judge of the underworld.

Immediately after Michelangelo's death, however, the campaign succeeded to some extent, and the minor artist Daniele da Volterra was commissioned to cover the genitals of Michelangelo's heroic males with *perizomas* or briefs. These alterations remain, despite the recent restoration of the chapel.

BAROQUE AND ROCOCO ART IN EUROPE

One of the most influential figures in the Counter Reformation fight-back against

Protestantism was St Ignatius of Loyola (1491–1556), the founder of the Jesuit Order. Loyola's *Spiritual Exercises*, written during 1522–24, had an enormous long-term influence over the direction taken by religious art in Europe, though that influence was not fully felt until a generation or more after his death.

The *Exercises* have for major themes: the experience of sin, the life of Jesus, the Passion of Jesus and the Resurrection of Jesus. It was the third of these themes that had the greatest impact on the visual arts, as the worshipper was encouraged to identify himself or herself as closely as possible with the physical sufferings of Christ.

The rarefied, almost abstract intellectualism of the last phase of Mannerism was followed by a brief phase of robust naturalism, identified now with the work of Caravaggio (1571–1610) but also with the early work of Annibale Carracci (1560–1609), and then by the fully developed Baroque style that dominated European painting and sculpture for the best part of a century, and which remained influential for much longer than that.

Essentially, the way in which the Baroque differs from what preceded it, especially in religious works, is not simply through its exaggeratedly vigorous forms, but because of the way in which the paintings and sculptures invite the closest empathy with the event portrayed. The spectator feels the wounds, experiences the physical sufferings of Christ and the saints, through the contemplation of art. The narrative of the Passion, and parallel narratives of

Christian martyrdom, especially the martyrdom of male saints, put frequent stress
on the idea of nudity. The nude figure is
vulnerable; the nude figure is humiliated;
the nude figure is also triumphant and
heroic amid suffering. Christ flagellated,
Christ on the Cross, St Sebastian shot full of
arrows, St Lawrence roasting on his grid-
iron—all of these, when portrayed by
Baroque artists, embody a new attitude to
the body. The spectator is no longer just an
observer; he lives inside the body he sees
depicted. Its agonies are his own agonies.
The result is an extraordinarily sensual art,
with strong sado-masochistic overtones. In
Baroque *Flagellations* the torture of Christ
becomes a perverted act of love, with strong
emphasis on the muscular physiques not
only of the executioners, but on that of
Christ himself. The tradition was so power-

ful that it persisted long after the Baroque era had passed.

One of the most powerfully erotic representations of the subject is by the nineteenth-century French academic painter William-Adolphe Bouguereau, painted as late as 1880. As in so many images of this sort, the loincloth given to Christ 'decently' veils his genitalia yet at the same time contrives both to suggest their form and to exaggerate their possible size. As it happens, this use of concealing yet symbolic drapery is a constant theme in Christian art—one that is explored in Leo Steinberg's classic book-length study, *The Sexuality of Christ in Renaissance Art and in Modern Oblivion*, first published in 1983. Steinberg's paradoxical argument is that artists regarded the exposure of Christ's genitalia (when he is shown as an infant), or calling attention to his sexual parts by other means, chiefly by the arrangement of drapery, as an affirmation of kinship with the human condition.

Whether or not one accepts this, it is certainly true to say that the use of skimpy draperies in Passion scenes and in martyrdoms more often than not calls attention to things that the intricate folds of cloth are, in theory, meant to conceal. And these draperies often seem to take on forms that are not only totally improbable in themselves, but which somehow mimic the shapes they are supposed to keep hidden.

Even where Baroque art is not religious, it has a powerful, empathetic physicality that carries the representation of nude or semi-nude figures beyond the boundaries of what had already been

The Flagellation of Our Lord Jesus Christ (1880) by William-Adolphe Bouguereau.

achieved in Western art, though certain aspects of this had already been foreshadowed in works from Hellenistic antiquity, such as the reliefs on the Great Altar of Pergamon, now in Berlin, and the Laocoon group in the Vatican. In battle scenes by Rubens, the combatants have muscles piled upon muscles—the spectator identifies with their awareness of their own strength just as much as he does with the physical agonies of the whipped or crucified Christ.

Rubens's celebrated portrait of his young second wife, Helene Fourment (1636–39, Kunsthistorisches Museum, Vienna), wearing nothing but a fur-lined pelisse that only very inadequately conceals her abundant flesh, is another example of this manipulation of the viewer's subjectivity. Though the garment does, indeed, partly hide the model's nudity, and in this sense 'censors' what is shown, at the same time, it powerfully suggests the way the luxurious cloak caresses the body it covers. Looking at the painting, we have a physical encounter with what it shows that goes beyond sight. We touch it, caress it, become part of it.

The artists of the Baroque period also had a keen awareness, shared with their contemporaries, of human mortality. Western art had already, in the late Middles Ages and in the Renaissance, produced works that expressed feelings of horror about the dissolution of the body. Among the best known are The Rohan Master's terrifying depiction of *Man Before His Judge* (c.1410–40, Bibliothéque nationale, Paris), and Hans Holbein's image of the *Dead Christ* (1521, Öffentliche

Kunstsammlung, Basle). Rembrandt pushes matters further in his *Anatomy Lesson of Dr Tulp* (1632, Mauritshuis, Den Haag). Here, the corpse being pored over by a group of learned men is a completely humiliated object—in no sense glorified, its sensual attraction brutally removed. This way of depicting the body can also be interpreted as a form of censorship. It warns us off the subject, rather than attempting to lure us in.

Parallels to this attitude to the body can be found in the art of our own time, for example in some of Francis Bacon's nudes, in Andres Serrano's photographs of corpses taken in morgues and in the French painter Jean Rustin's images of naked geriatrics.

As the religious fervour of the seventeenth century waned and the Baroque became the Rococo, religious painting tended

The Rohan Master's *Man Before His Judge*.

more and more to find itself displaced by secular themes. In the eighteenth century there was a strong revival of the erotic representations that had once been associated with Mannerist court painters, though now with a prurient overtone associated with the idea of virginity and the loss of virginity. One artist who made a specialty of symbolic paintings celebrating, or, to speak more accurately, hypocritically lamenting this loss was the Frenchman Jean-Baptiste Greuze, author of paintings such as *The Broken Jug* (1772, Louvre, Paris), which uses a simple symbol, a young girl who has broken a clay jug when going to fill it at a fountain, to epitomize the situation. What makes works of this kind erotic is not what is shown—the single figure remains fully clothed—but what is suggested.

In Greuze's day, his fervent defender was the great Encyclopaedist Denis Diderot (1713–84), though Diderot had started to abandon his protégé a little before *The Broken Jug* was painted. What attracted Diderot to Greuze was the apparent 'simplicity' and 'honesty' of his sentiments, as opposed to the corruption and artificiality prevalent at the French court. In contrast to this, Diderot detested the work of François Boucher, a great favourite with Mme de Pompadour, the mistress of Louis XV, and with the court circle in general.

The situation was, however, more complicated than Diderot liked to believe, and raises questions that are very relevant to the theme of this essay: the way in which we censor representations of the human body. Images of children pose especially difficult questions for a twenty-first century audience.

Our society is marked by an obsession
with and often an acute panic about paedophilia—that is to say, sexual feelings pro-
jected on to pubescent and pre-pubescent
children. At a time when children matured
earlier, married earlier and were often producing children of their own when still in
their mid-teens, this panic did not exist in
the same form. Yet it is also clear that adolescent bodies, even in much earlier times,
aroused a sexual response that we would
now recognize as paedophilic. Greuze's
'virginity' pictures—*The Broken Jug* is only
the best known of a whole series—focus on
the sexuality of young girls. Also, a
number of celebrated Renaissance and
post-Renaissance paintings and sculptures
pick up a theme from classical Greek art
and focus on the sexual allure of adolescent
boys. Two famous examples are Donatello's

David (1439, Museo Nazionale del Bargello, Florence) and Caravaggio's *St John the Baptist with a Ram* (1601/1602, Capitoline Museum, Rome).

These masterpieces are protected from censure—and from censorship—by their celebrity, and also by their long-established position as key works in the history of Western art. One has to acknowledge, however, that forthright 'new' versions of the same subjects, perhaps expressed through the medium of photography, would, almost certainly, in a contemporary context, attract attempts at suppression.

One can, however, take the argument further than this. One striking characteristic of Rococo art, particularly in France, is its tendency to present the chief actors in erotic and/or mythological scenes as chubby adolescents, rather than as fully mature, though still youthful, men and women. This tendency manifests itself in a number of typical works by Boucher. For example, when Venus demands arms for the hero Aeneas from the reluctant Smith God Vulcan in *The Visit of Venus to Vulcan* (1754, Wallace Collection, London), Vulcan, far from being shown as a mature, heavily muscled craftsman, is portrayed as a sulky nude teenager.

The cult of childhood can be said to have begun in the eighteenth century, under the influence of the philosopher Jean-Jacques Rousseau (1712–78). His basic ideas on child education are set out in his didactic novel *Emile*, published in 1762. In this, he makes it clear that in his opinion children up to the age of 12 are no better than little animals. Despite this, he set in train a celebration of childhood as a condition very different from, and in some respects superior to, full adulthood that continues to have great impact today. Contingent on Rousseau's theories are many of our ideas about permissible ways of representing children as physical beings.

THE NINETEENTH CENTURY

The nineteenth century is still close enough to us for many of the issues we still have about the representation of the human body to be present in images from that period. One of the things that drastically influenced, and continues to influence, attitudes was the invention of photography. Most seminal inventions have to make their way little by little, gradually displacing what is familiar, as the 'horseless carriage' displaced the horse-drawn conveyances that at first it resembled and evolved into the automobile. Photography, by contrast, had been long-awaited in a world that was impatient to find a way of making permanent the images produced by the *camera oscura*. However, it was also, at its beginnings, the subject of misunderstandings. For early users, it was a purely objective medium, through which whatever the camera saw could be directly recorded. It was only gradually, as the medium became more sophisticated, that people came to realize how much the image was affected by the sensibility of the photographer.

Invented at a moment when there was a strong Evangelical religious revival taking place, photography seemed to some early enthusiasts to be a means that the deity had provided in order to make artists superfluous. This is the significance of the title that the British photographic pioneer William Henry Fox Talbot (1800–77) chose for his book *The Pencil of Nature* (1842–44), which was the first publication to be illustrated with photographs.

When pioneer photographers turned their cameras on human beings, as opposed to still lifes or landscapes, they were immediately confronted with the wide difference between most human individuals and the inherited classical ideal. These differences became especially conspicuous when they made images of the male or female nude.

In terms of their psychological impact, photographs of the nude differ from paintings, drawings or sculptures of the nude in one extremely significant way. With images made by traditional means, one is free to imagine that what one sees comes largely from the artist's own head—that is, from the region behind the eyes rather than from directly in front of them. In the case of a photograph, no such pretence is possible—it insists on the physical presence of an observer, as well as that of the thing that is observed. In other words, photographs of the nude always offer proof of a voyeuristic situation. Not surprisingly, given the constraints of nineteenth-century morality, this made a large part of the nineteenth-century audience feel extremely uneasy, the more so because photography rapidly became a democratic medium, which made it possible to disseminate images of all kinds well beyond the boundaries of an elite audience.

Not surprisingly, photography rapidly took on a powerful role as a creator of erotic images that enjoyed a huge clandestine circulation. In this sense, it offers an instance of a process that has continued into the twenty-first century, and which shows no sign of coming to an end. An image-making technology linked to the basic erotic impulse has increasingly large financial resources at its disposal, and financial resources drive forward technical innovation. If we look at the successive developments in image-making technology that have taken place in our own time, among them Polaroid photography, the hand-held video camera and the digital camera, one notes that a large part of their commercial success has been due to the fact that they put the ability to make erotic images within reach of everyone, without fear of censorship.

Nineteenth-century erotic photography
had not yet reached this stage—nearly all of
it was the work of professional studios,
working with or without the connivance of
the authorities, in theory in defiance of the
law, but very often able to flout it. However,
this vast production of erotic images has
one characteristic that we are now inclined
to forget—the audience, for it was almost
entirely male. That is, where material of
this sort was concerned, there was a censorship by gender. This division had existed
earlier, but seems to have been much less
rigid. The erotic paintings created for
princely patrons were visible to all who frequented courtly circles. Religious paintings
with a strong erotic charge were intended
to make their impact, not upon solitary
worshippers, but on whole congregations.

To some extent this censorship still exists, though in a new form. It is noticeable that many feminists are hostile to erotic representations, and particularly photographic ones, because they regard them as things that exploit women and, in particular, as things that enshrine male efforts to control women and reduce them to subservient status.

In addition to nineteenth-century photographs of the nude whose purpose was purely erotic, there were others whose purpose was either scientific or, at least by announced intention, 'artistic'. Among the best-known scientific photographs are those made by Eadweard Muybridge (1830–1904). An Englishman who established himself in California, Muybridge, with the financial support of the wealthy race-horse owner Leland Stanford, began a series of photographic studies of horses, designed to prove that at certain times, when galloping, they had all four feet off the ground. These studies were later extended to human beings—males, females, even a crippled child. They gave an entirely new idea about how the human body functioned and how it moved from one position to another. The figures were shown entirely nude, without covering of any kind, so that the action being studied could be seen as clearly as possible.

Muybridge's photographs were never thought of as questionable by their original audience—they were, in any case, first published in expensive editions. Yet, much later, Francis Bacon was to find in some of them material for paintings that are decidedly erotic.

Almost from its beginnings, photography was thought of as something that could provide useful reference material for artists. Among the best-known examples of this are the photographs of nudes that the ageing Delacroix commissioned from his friend Eugene Durieu (1800–74). Yet the situation of these 'art' photographs of the nude was ambiguous in more than one way. It is clear, for example, that most of the photographs published 'for the use of artists' were in fact attempts to feed the market for erotica with material that could be thought of as being at least marginally legitimate. It is also clear that these photographs increasingly represent an effort to force the photographic image to conform to existing prototypes in painting and sculpture. These efforts almost inevitably failed.

Some interesting sidelights concerning nineteenth-century attitudes towards the body and its representation can be found in the career of the celebrated German-born strongman Eugene Sandow (1867–1925). Sandow became a major Victorian celebrity, thanks very largely to the almost-nude photographs of him that circulated in huge numbers. He ranks, in fact, as the first male pin-up.

In these images, Sandow sometimes wears a gymnast's costume, or is got up as the Greek demi-god Hercules with a leopard skin loincloth. In many, he is almost completely naked, with an artificial fig-leaf clipped to his penis, in order to hide his genital area. This adornment inevitably draws the eye to exactly the area that it is supposed to avoid. It also, for anyone who

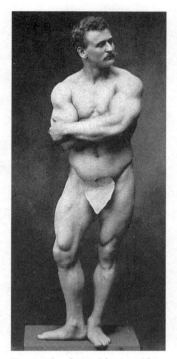

Eugene Sandow, with an artificial fig-leaf clipped to his penis.

Eugene Sandow, posing against a pillar.

has a familiarity with Greek and Roman sculpture, often thus censored in modern times, emphasizes the difference between the way Sandow's body was constructed, as the product of some of the first modern scientific body-building techniques, and the genuinely classical ideal.

The social necessity of concealing the male genitalia was, of course, something that troubled both painters and sculptors for centuries. Seventeenth-, eighteenth- and nineteenth-century post-classical sculptures with heroic themes offer a truly comic panorama of different devices, each less convincing than the last. Fig leaves are no longer sufficient—there are innumerable scarves and sashes that defy the laws of gravity, clinging as if magnetized to the offending part. Perhaps my favourite example is a work by the minor sculptor

Jean-Pierre Cortot (1787–1843) now in the Louvre. This represents a warrior in his death agony—*The Soldier from Marathon Announcing Victory* (1834). He falls to the ground, face contorted, one arm triumphantly upraised. Round his penis and testicles there coils an elaborate ribbon, seemingly with a life of its own, whose presence has nothing to do with the subject of the sculpture. Like Sandow's artificial fig-leaf, it efficiently directs one's gaze to precisely the detail that one is not supposed to notice.

Yet surrounding works in the same sculpture court, from precisely the same epoch, make it clear that the policy of concealment was never consistent. Next door to Cortot's *Soldier* stands a group by his slightly older contemporary François-

Ribbon detail from *The Soldier from Marathon Announcing Victory* (1834) by Jean-Pierre Cortot.

Joseph Bosio (1768–1845) representing
Hercules Fighting Achelous (1824). Hercules
is stark naked and, if anything, slightly
over-endowed.

It is worth dwelling on nineteenth-century sculpture for a little longer, since two
of the most famous artistic controversies of
that time were aroused by nude sculptures.
One is *Woman Bitten by a Snake* by Jean-
Baptiste Clésinger (1814–83) now in the
Musée d'Orsay, Paris. This caused a scandal
when it was exhibited in the Salon of 1847
because many spectators thought it had
been moulded from life. The same accusa-
tion was made, 30 years later, against
Auguste Rodin's (1840–1917) male nude
The Age of Bronze (1877). Looking at either
of these now, the notion seems ludicrous.
Both have a consistent stylistic language to-

tally at odds with the notion of a literal body-cast—of the kind made from Eugene Sandow's body by the Natural History Museum in London. This was such a disappointment that the Museum soon hid it away—it remains in store and can only be seen by special request. Interestingly, this 'scientific' effort is the direct forerunner of the Super Realist sculptures of the nude made in the 1970s by the US artist John de Andrea (b.1941).

The controversies I have just mentioned are, nevertheless, instructive in retrospect, as they indicate something that the two sculptures have in common, which is their inclination to break away from established classical conventions. They both spring from a renewed examination of the human body, an object to be looked at directly, as a thing existing in its own right, rather than obliquely, through reference to art history. The more closely one looks at nineteenth-century art, the more clearly one tends to see that the representation of the body, more especially the nude body, depended on a whole series of unspoken agreements between artists and the society that surrounded and supported them. The comedy of draperies, ribbons and fig-leaves that I have just described played a very small part in all this, but it was nevertheless symptomatic. Photography of the nude was subversive, not only because of its un-doubted erotic charge, but because, despite all its attempts to conform to established artistic conventions, it offered inescapable truths about appearances that had never previously been available in such a completely stable form.

One important way in which
nineteenth-century art censored representation of the body was by insisting on an
element of 'otherness' in images of the
nude. The easiest way to achieve this was by
making references to classicism. A carica-
ture by the great satirist Honoré Daumier
(1808–79) put the situation very neatly. It
showed two visitors to the annual French
Salon—over-dressed *bourgeoises*—one of
whom is saying disapprovingly to the other:
'This year, it's Venuses once again.' The
Salons, frequented by enormous numbers of
people, needed controversy to bring in
visitors. It was, nevertheless, controversy
within strict limits, where both sides re-
spected certain boundaries. Only very occa-
sionally did artists step over the line. When
Edouard Manet (1832–83) showed his nude
Olympia in the Salon of 1865, it aroused

'This year, it's Venuses once again.'

extraordinary outrage not because of the subject itself—the painting was a paraphrase of the *Venus of Urbino*, no more and no less provocative than Titian's original—but because the model had been subtly transformed into a contemporary Parisian woman, gazing boldly out of the canvas, untroubled by public nudity. Tellingly, the public jumped to the conclusion that this was a representation of a *demi-mondaine*. Her nudity shocked them less than her supposed profession. While it is true that Manet offered a few clues—chief among them the black maid in the background who presents a bouquet—the spectator essentially constructed the situation for himself (or herself), projecting on to the image things s/he already knew about the society s/he lived in.

Another way of achieving the required
degree of distance was to show the naked
body in some exotic setting, preferably
Middle Eastern. Perhaps the best-known
artist to employ this theme was Jean-
Auguste-Dominique Ingres (1780–1867),
whose final masterpiece was *The Turkish
Bath* of 1862. It was also popular with
others, among them the dedicated oppo-
nent of the Impressionists, Jean-Léon
Gérôme (1824–1904). Gérôme painted
bath scenes, harem scenes and slave mar-
kets. The paintings in the final category are
particularly significant, as they stress not
merely otherness but the idea of female
subjugation. The nude female is shown as
shamed and humiliated, but the blame for
her situation is neatly shifted, from the
painter, from the Western spectator (who is
in this instance the painter's surrogate), to

Slave Market (1866) by Jean-Léon Gérôme.

male protagonists in the alien milieu where
the chief subject of the painting had been
placed. Slave-market compositions act out
negative feelings about nudity, generated
by Christian guilt, while at the same time
allowing a full view of the nude itself. It is,
however, a significant feature of these
slave-market scenes that they omit certain
details. When the female slave appears in a
fully frontal pose her pubis is always per-
fectly smooth, no trace of a vagina and no
pubic hair. This is true of nineteenth-
century Salon nudes in general, whatever
the announced subject.

THE MODERN MOVEMENT

The photography of the late-nineteenth
and early-twentieth centuries made its own

contribution to the idea of 'otherness'.
Where painters of the exotic tended to focus
on the Middle East, a subject of interest
ever since Napoleon's Egyptian campaign
of 1806, itinerant photographers wandered
more widely, recording the colonial posses-
sions of the leading European powers,
many of them very recently acquired.
There was a fascination not only with local
scenery and architecture but also with the
inhabitants of these unfamiliar territories—
their way of life and their customary dress.
In tribal Africa, where many women
appeared in public bare to the waist,
photographers found images that aroused
prurient interest in Europe. Though
European painters were relatively slow to
embrace African subject-matter, there
were, by the end of the nineteenth century,
a large number of photographic postcards

in circulation showing semi-clothed African women. These escaped censure because of their supposed 'scientific' value, as things that offered information about unfamiliar areas of the globe. They also served to confirm European feelings of superiority. Bare-breasted African women, it was felt, lived in a morally less complex situation than the Europeans who bought and looked at the postcards.

Recent research into the genesis of Picasso's *Demoiselles d'Avignon* (1911, Museum of Modern Art, New York), a key work in the history of the Modern Movement, indicates that postcards of this type were among the source material used by the artist, and that the painting owes almost as much to these images as it does to the African tribal carvings that are its long-ac-

cepted major source. In fact, what inter-
ested Picasso was exactly the feeling of otherness that he located in the photographs
as well as in the carvings. Different as these
were from one another, what united them
in Picasso's imagination was not simply
their common origin in Africa, but the
sense of radical alienation, of divorce from
anything familiar, that both sets of images
conveyed. The ironic title given to the
work—it refers not to the city of Avignon
but to the girls in a low-class brothel in the
Calle d'Avignon in Barcelona—reflects this
sense of a violent divorce from an inherited
ideal.

If one looks at the major art move-
ments that dominated the early years of
Modernism—Fauvism, Expressionism, Cu-
bism, Futurism and Surrealism—one of the

things that they all have in common is a
tendency to distort and fragment the
human body. The tendency had its roots in
many places. One, certainly, was increasing
interest in so-called 'primitive' art, with its
tendency to represent body parts, and the
relationship between these parts, in joltingly
symbolic rather than naturalistic ways. Yet
this was not the whole story—the Modernists wanted to break down familiar ways
of seeing, and to endow customary subject
matter with a new emotional charge.

Where the audience had previously
been alarmed by works of art that seemed
to stick too closely to the physical facts, it
was now alarmed by art that seemed to vio-
late the human body. The new art increasingly used sexual reference as a means of
forcing spectators out of their comfort zone

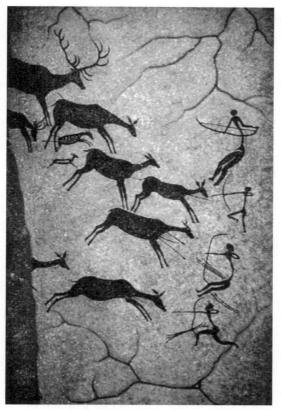

Bowmen and Reindeer—primitive art from Los Caballos,
Spain.

and of forcing them to engage with the work. In particular, this became a tactic associated with the artists of the Surrealist Movement, who owed a substantial debt to Sigmund Freud.

In one sense, this was simply an extension of a tactic already familiar to the Salon artists of the nineteenth century, whose work, as I have already noted, provoked quite frequent controversies stemming from differing ideas about how the body, and in particular the unclothed body, should be represented in art. In another sense, as the bourgeois audience clearly understood, it was a direct attack on the existing social order. What could be more radical than trying to subvert the spectator's sense of himself as a physical being?

The first half of the twentieth century was marked by the hostility of two major dictatorships—Nazi and Soviet—to the Modern Movement in art. In large part, this seems to have been fuelled by the way in which Modernist artists seemed to distort representations of the human body. This was certainly one of the themes of the *En-tarte Kunst* (Degenerate Art) exhibition staged by the Nazis in Munich in 1937. The show later travelled to 11 more cities in Germany and Austria, and was seen by an estimated three million visitors, more people than any other exhibition of Modernist art held up to that time. Everything possible was done to demean the paintings and sculptures on view, and to make them look ridiculous. The effect was reinforced by slogans painted on the walls:

'Insolent mockery of the Divine
under Centrist rule'

'Revelation of the Jewish racial soul'

'An insult to German womanhood'

'The ideal—cretin and whore'

'Even museum bigwigs called this
the "art of the German people"'

For the Nazis, the opposite of *Entarte
Kunst*, the ideal to which art ought to as-
pire, was the Heroic, by which they meant
the Romantic Realist style inherited from
the nineteenth century, stiffened with a
good dose of Neo-classicism. This style can
be seen at its most typical in the sculptures
that one of Hitler's favourite artists, Arno
Breker (1900–91) provided for the new
Reich Chancellery in Berlin. However,
Breker was not simply an artist whom the
Nazis admired. He belonged to the world-

wide return to classical values in art that
flourished between the wars. Even Picasso
was touched by this impulse, as can be seen
from the etchings of the Vollard Suite,
made between 1930 and 1937, which paraphrase the classicism of Ingres, an artist
whom Picasso always greatly admired. During part of the 1920s, Breker lived in Paris,
where he got to know Aristide Maillol
(1861–1944). Maillol admired Breker's
work, which had certain things in common
with his own sculpture, and went so far as to
describe him as 'the German Michelangelo'.

Soviet Socialist Realist art had a similar
fascination with classical values, often diluted
with things borrowed from French Impres-
sionism. Its typical subjects—portraits of
Lenin and Stalin, images of heroic proletari-
ans (a good example is Vera Mukhina's 25-
metre-tall sculptural group, *Labourer and*

Kolkhoz Woman, created for the Paris *Exposition Internationale* of 1937)—fitted easily into this formula. Yet, it is also worth remembering that many typical Socialist Realist compositions had deep roots in the art of the Wanderers, a Russian late-nineteenth-century artistic group that aimed to democratize art and bring it to the people.

Essentially, both the Modernists and their opponents censored representation of the human body to suit their own ideological purposes. In this respect, they were no different from the artists of many preceding generations. It is also important to note that the desire to control art, and in particular the way the body was shown, was not an invention of the twentieth-century dictatorships. Almost every governing authority of which we have record has tried to impose its own ideas on artists, forbidding some things and perhaps accepting others. And these demands have always had a particular focus on the way in which the human body was represented. To control the human image was the magical equivalent of exerting control over the great mass of the ruled.

THE PARTICULAR VERSUS THE UNIVERSAL

The Weimar period in Germany was significant for several reasons. It witnessed a fierce ideological struggle between Nazis, Communists and liberals, offering a picture of a society under extreme stress. It also, with the Bauhaus, pioneered a new way of looking at the relationships between art and technology.

One of the things that the Nazi ideologists hated most in the art of the Weimar Republic were the paintings made by artists such as George Grosz (1893–1959) and Otto Dix (1891–1969) that highlighted the decadence of Weimar society and its apparently limitless sexual freedom. Yet the artists also saw that this freedom was, in economic terms, a kind of slavery, because many women had been forced into prostitution by the financial crisis that followed Germany's defeat in the First World War.

Even more than this, they hated the images made by the same artists that recorded the plight of those who had been hideously mutilated by the war. The style practised by these artists derived to some extent from the Expressionist movement that had flourished in Germany during the immediately pre-War period. What was different, post-

War, was that the artists increasingly aban-
doned Expressionist subjectivity in favour
of a cold-eyed assessment of contemporary
reality. This earned their work a stylistic
label—the New Objectivity.

This commitment to detached observation of the contemporary world, often in its
most hideous aspects, owed a lot to the
progress of photography. Photography had
now become the primary means of recording the world. Photographic images, rather
than paintings or sculptures, were the most
immediate point of reference when people
considered what they saw, and looked for
some kind of objective correlative that
would confirm their own observations.

To make a small but important point, it
was photographs of the mutilated, often
made for scientific reasons, which fixed
their plight inescapably in the public mind.

As I have already noted, it is one of the characteristics of photography that it seems to offer a guarantee that the event, person or thing represented in a photograph possesses a quite separate existence from the photograph itself. The same thing cannot be said with perfect confidence about what is shown in a painting.

If one makes a leap forward, past the Second World War, to a survey of the development of both art and photography during the second half of the twentieth century, one sees that it is essentially photography and its derivatives that are now the battlegrounds where the struggle for the control of the human image is fought out. Once again, there is more than one reason for this, and some of those reasons have very little to do with what we speak of as 'art'.

In order to understand why this is the case, one has to take at least a brief look at the development of contemporary art during the 60 years or so that have passed since the end of the Second World War.

To put matters very simply, the victory of the Allies consecrated the Modern Movement and began a process through which this surrendered its outsider status and became the official, and officially supported, art of the United States and the Western democracies in Europe and, later, throughout more or less the whole world. The culmination of this was the collapse of the Soviet Union and of the Soviet regimes in Eastern Europe, and the emergence of a new market-oriented culture in China after the death of Chairman Mao and the end of the Cultural Revolution.

The new contemporary art brought
with it, as part of the DNA it had inherited
from the original Modernists, the presumption that a truly valid and creative art had
to be controversial—in other words, that it
had to challenge inherited values and, with
them, the *status quo*. However, if one analy-
ses this challenge, as exemplified in key
early-Modernist works, one discovers that it
was not unitary. There were at least three
areas of controversy, not always closely re-
lated to one another, rather than just one.

The first area was to do with the way
the external world was perceived, and how
these perceptions were to be rendered in
art. Some Modernists contended that the
artist need not, in fact, refer to the external
world at all: art could be a completely
closed system, sufficient unto itself. This led
to the birth of abstraction and eventually

culminated in the Minimalism of the 1970s, which seemed to mark the end of a linear progression that had begun with the appearance of the *Fauves* in 1905. After that, Modernism became Post-Modernism.

Though the movement towards abstraction played a prominent role in the development of the Modernist sensibility, not all—not even a majority—of Modernist artists wanted to make abstract work. A good many wanted to radically reconfigure what was seen, while still leaving the subject more or less recognizable. The established audience for art—the direct descendants of those people who had frequented the great nineteenth-century Salons in such numbers—often felt threatened by this, especially threatened, perhaps, when what was being reconfigured was the human body, and often exploded in anger.

Since the new art was seen by many people as subversive, it was naturally, but at first illogically, linked to the idea of political subversion, even though there was no organic connection. It was the radical artists who seized on the idea that what they were producing ought to be politically engaged. This engagement was not, however, inherent in their work, but was, instead, something that came afterwards. The earliest art movement to become politicized was Italian Futurism, and the Futurists were not men of the Left, but of the radical Right. The prophet of the movement, the poet and polemicist F. T. Marinetti (1876–1944), was later to ally himself with Mussolini's Fascism.

Soviet Communism was originally supported by the leading members of the Russ-

ian Modernist avant-garde, but this alliance
very soon turned sour. Socialist Realism was
officially imposed by Stalin in 1932 when
he issued an official directive 'On the Re-
construction of Literary and Art Organiza-
tions'. Even before this, the avant-garde in
Russia had been steadily losing ground,
and a number of leading progressive artists,
among them Marc Chagall (1887–1985),
had gone into exile.

The relationship between the inter-War
avant-garde and the official Left is best
examined through the strenuous but un-
availing efforts made by the Surrealist
Movement, under the leadership of André
Breton (1896–1966), to ally itself with Russian Communism. These efforts failed, and
the Surrealists became Trotskyists, more or
less.

The third area where the Modernist avant-garde insisted on its radical credentials was in its attitude to sexuality and through its use of sexually charged images. Yet, as I have already suggested, this tactic was not novel: it had been employed by artists throughout the nineteenth century and sexual scandals were a regular feature of the annual Paris Salons.

If we look at the situation as it exists today, we immediately see that the reconfiguration of ways in which the external world is represented is no longer a live issue. The audience is inured, the system of patronage accepts any such efforts as a matter of course—our 'grammar of seeing' will accept more or less anything that contemporary artists choose to throw at us.

It is also more or less taken for granted that artists should regularly profess radical views about society and its ills. These views are now shared, though not perhaps always so passionately embraced, by the majority of the politically liberal audience that frequents the major museums of contemporary art and visits the ever increasing number of art *biennales*. The political discourse of art that aspires to be avant-garde is thus very much a matter of preaching to the converted. Despite the success of Joseph Beuys (1921–86) in using both museums and recurring major art events such as the Cassel Documenta as platforms for the dissemination of minority political views, the combination of politics and art has in general tended to undercut the seriousness of the intended political discourse. To put it bluntly, this is because officially sponsored displays of contemporary art have now found a comfortable place in our

society as a form of popular entertainment—one that excites curiosity, wonder
and ridicule in about equal measure.

This leaves the question of sexual representation. Here two things are noticeable.
The first is that the sexual content of art
that aspires to be avant-garde has become
more and more extreme. Formerly taboo
subjects, such as homosexuality, co-
prophilia, the sexual allurer of bodily de-
formity and the conjunction of sex and
death all feature in officially sponsored
exhibitions staged in major institutions.
Sometimes there are protests, and the cry
of 'censorship' immediately goes up. Very
rarely are these protests successful—they
serve chiefly to reinforce the avant-garde's
sense of its own righteous invulnerability.
Meanwhile, the publicity generated by

these predictable controversies brings even more visits to the events concerned. In fact, the basic mechanism continues to work in the same way as it did in the nineteenth century.

The thing that is different, however, is the role played by photography and by its close relations, film and video. The majority of the contemporary artists most obviously committed to sexual shock— examples are Robert Mapplethorpe, Joel-Peter Witkin (b.1939), Andres Serrano (b.1950), Gilbert and George (Gilbert Proesch [b.1943] and George Passmore [b.1942])—make use of photographic means. This leads one to reflect on the role played by modern high-technology imaging techniques in situations where there can be no possibility that the image has an artistic intention. When image-making leaves the shelter of the museum, the situation shifts in disconcerting ways.

There was a time, now increasingly remote, when all forms of image-making could be defined as 'art'. There was no distinction, as there was from the very beginning with the use of language, between what was constructed with an artistic intention and what wasn't. The invention of photography put an end to this, more especially when the photograph could be linked to various means of mechanical reproduction and be multiplied at will. Now, visual images, just as much as words, are the common currency of communication in nearly all societies. They form so much part of our lives that we tend to forget that this was not a situation that existed 200 years ago.

In recent times, the technology of image-making has taken enormous strides. In any society with access to this technology—and that means in all of the industrialized nations—almost any individual can make detailed images of anything he or she chooses to portray, and disseminate them worldwide. It is not a situation that ever existed previously. It is not only that the whole process of image-making has been democratized, it is also that it has increasingly tended to escape from hierarchical control. All societies, even those that pride themselves on possessing fully democratic institutions, have a desire to control the flow of information, and images are now the most potent element in this flow.

Not surprisingly, one of the things that any person or institution laying claim to

authority most wishes to control is representations of the human body and, in particular, of the unclothed human body. My
reasons for making this assertion are im-
plicit in the admittedly highly compressed
account of the development of art that I
have given in this text. If we ask ourselves
why representations of the human form
have always been edited, sometimes in ways
that are completely contrary to what we
learn about it by using our own eyes, the
answer has to be, I think, that the body,
from the very beginnings of mankind, has
been a source of anxiety. With most other
forms of representation, we can at least
make an attempt to escape from our subjectivity. With representations of our own
flesh, we cannot do that.

The frequent appearance, in many cultures, of religious sanctions that control, or

even completely forbid, images of the nude should not be a surprise, as these can be interpreted as attempts to assuage the anxious feelings I have described. The universal nature of this unease seems to transcend wide differences in religious belief.

In secular societies, the anxiety becomes attached to particular causes or sets of ideas. This can produce surprising examples of intolerance. A celebrated feminist artist once told me how much she disliked the *Rokeby Venus* of Velazquez (1599–1660), now in the collection of the National Gallery in London. What she disliked about it was the fact that it seemed to her to encapsulate the idea of the 'controlling gaze'—the domination of women by male scopophilia—that is now an important component in feminist theory. I asked her

whether, in the unlikely event of her be-
coming the director of the gallery, she
would withdraw the painting from view.
The answer, though hedged about with
qualifications, seemed to be that she would.

A very pertinent case—one I have
already referred to earlier—is that of representations of nude children. Thanks to
current concerns about paedophilia, our
society increasingly tends to disapprove of,
and in many cases to suppress, images of
this sort. Police forces attempt to trace and
prosecute those who download material of
this type from the Internet. An unchal-
lengeable reason for this concern is that the
making of the images involves the exploita-
tion of the subjects—another example of
the fact that a photograph, unlike a painting, guarantees, or seems to guarantee, that
what it shows actually existed in reality.

Yet three points need to be made here. The first, already touched upon, is that a great deal of 'classic' art features precisely this category of subject-matter. Donatello's nude adolescent *David* has already been mentioned, but what about the revelling *putti* that adorn his *Cantoria* (1433–39) in the Florence Duomo? Not all of these are completely naked, but some of them are. Do they now run the risk of exciting impure thoughts in a sacred space, and should breeches be made for them, as was done for the nudes in Michelangelo's *Last Judgement*?

The second point is that our disapproval of these images, even those that are photographic, is much more recent than we care to recall. In the late-1960s and early-1970s, the days of 'flower power', there was a brief vogue for books with photographs of happily nude hippie families. Some of these photos featured bearded dads dandling their naked offspring on their knees. It is a safe bet that these could not be republished today.

The third point is obvious. Despite all legal obstacles, images of this type continue to circulate in large numbers, thanks chiefly to new technological means of communication. The impossibility of wholly suppressing them increases the amount of anxiety, and therefore anger, that they generate.

The instability of our attitudes towards the human body can be demonstrated in another fashion. Where feminism has led to increasing hostility towards images of the female nude, the campaign for homosexual equality has tended to raise the status of the male equivalent.

This change in status can be measured in two ways. The first is the steady rise to prominence of art with homosexual themes, even when these are presented in a brutally erotic way, as they are in many of the photographs of Robert Mapplethorpe (1946–89). Images of this sort are thought of as being transgressive in a 'good' way— our acceptance of them is a celebration of our own tolerance and of our awareness of the need to be cutting edge, in tune with the way our society is developing. The second, maybe even more significant, is the process whereby artists and photographers who were till recently regarded as total outsiders—among them the photographer Bruce of Los Angeles (Bruce Bellas, 1909–74) and the gleefully pornographic homosexual illustrator Tom of Finland (Touko Laaksonen, 1920–91)—have been co-opted

into the pantheon of high art. Neither of
them would have expected this honour.
Both thought the primary purpose of their
work was to provide erotic entertainment
for a specialized audience. Representations
of the female nude, on the other hand, are
increasingly regarded as kitsch, and the
days when the US pin-up could be celebrated in avant-garde art have long gone.

Whenever people explore the question
of what should and should not be permit-
ted, where representations of the body are
concerned, they make an appeal to morality or, failing that, simply to the idea of
decorum. The presumption, in both cases,
is that everyone knows what morality is, or
at least what can be regarded as decorous.
The most cursory examination of human
history, or even of the different societies that

exist today, shows that no assumption could
be less well founded. We may wish for moral
absolutes, or absolute rules of conduct, but
all the evidence is against us. The one constant, inherited from our remotest past, is
the state of anxiety I have already described.
The psychic tensions it sets up have been
inherited in an ever-more complex form by
modern society. Representations of the
human body will, for the foreseeable future,
remain a battleground, fought over by liber-
tarians and anti-libertarians. The irony is
that those who think of themselves as liber-
tarians will frequently be tempted to cross
over to the other side. 'Politically correct',
the phrase often used when this transforma-
tion takes place, is, after all, just a euphe-
mism for censorship.